Divine Divas

Costume & Design Adult Coloring Book

Betty Ann Fraley

Illume Writers & Artists

ISBN: 978-1515361688

Illume Writers & Artists
PO Box 86, Gilbertsville, NY 13776

Printed in the United States of America

 **Cut out this page to use as backing, to prevent bleed-through to subsequent pages**

3

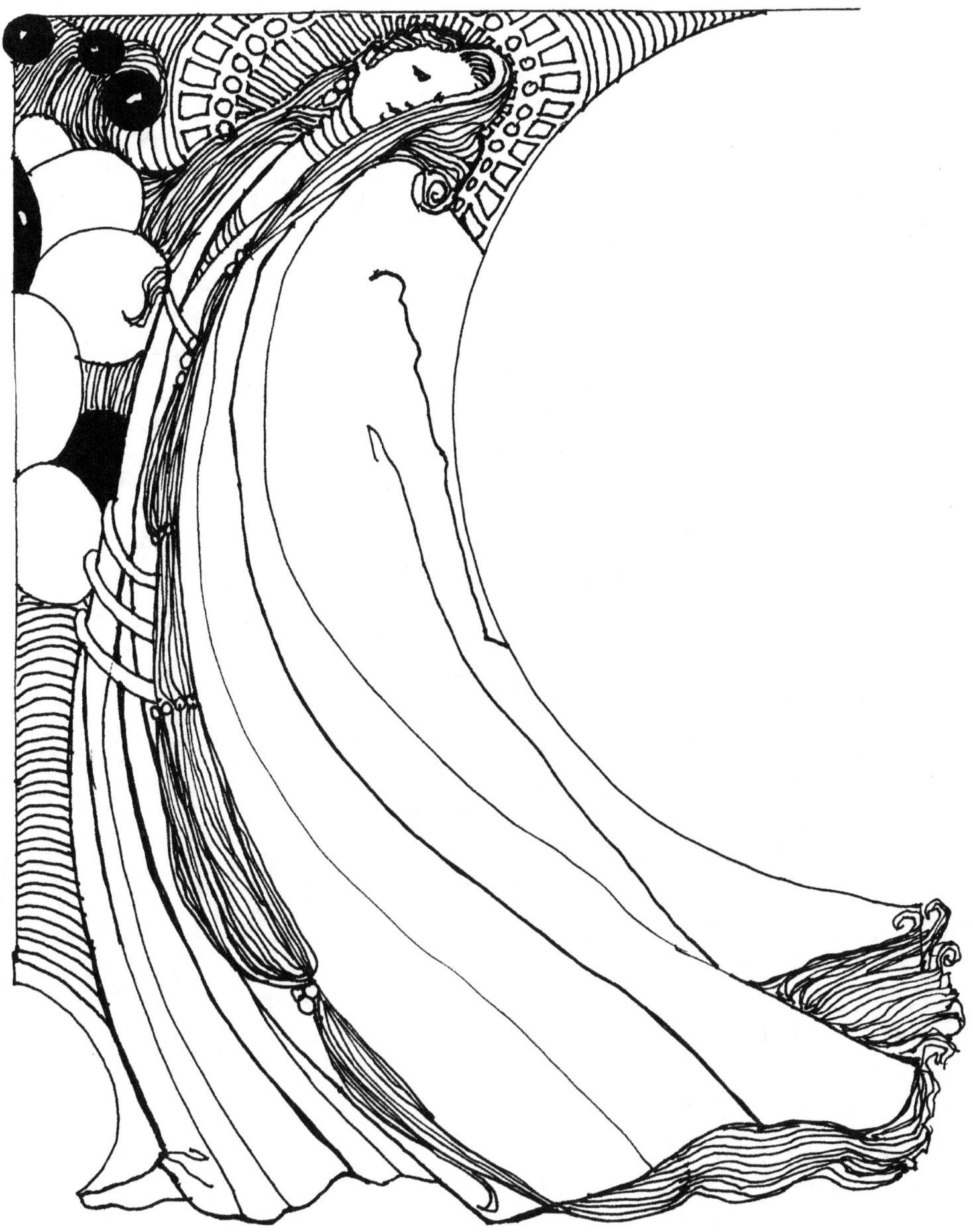

13

16

18

19